AFTER THE CLIMB

WHO DO YOU THINK YOU ARE?

KEISHA L. HUNTER

After The Climb © Copyright 2026 Keisha L. Hunter

All rights reserved. No part of this publication may be reproduced, distributed, or transmitted in any form or by any means, including photocopying, recording, or other electronic or mechanical methods, without the prior written permission of the publisher, except in the case of brief quotations embodied in critical reviews and certain other noncommercial uses permitted by copyright law.

Although the author and publisher have made every effort to ensure that the information in this book was correct at press time, the author and publisher do not assume and hereby disclaim any liability to any party for any loss, damage, or disruption caused by errors or omissions, whether such errors or omissions result from negligence, accident, or any other cause.

Adherence to all applicable laws and regulations, including international, federal, state, and local governing professional licensing, business practices, advertising, and all other aspects of doing business in the U.S., Canada, or any other jurisdiction, is the sole responsibility of the reader and consumer.

Neither the author nor the publisher assumes any responsibility or liability whatsoever on behalf of the consumer or reader of this material. Any perceived slight of any individual or organization is purely unintentional.

The resources in this book are provided for informational purposes only and should not be used to replace the specialized training and professional judgment of a health care or mental health care professional.

Neither the author nor the publisher can be held responsible for the use of the information provided within this book. Please always consult a trained professional before making any decision regarding treatment of yourself or others.

For more information, email keishahunter26@yahoo.com

ISBN: 979-8-90057-126-3 - Ebook

ISBN: 979-8-90057-127-0 - Paperback

ISBN: 979-8-90057-128-7 - Hardcover

Get Your Free Gift!

To get the best experience with your climb, I've found readers who download and use [Becoming A Content Creator] can generate income to support your vision and goals.

BUILD YOUR PASSIVE INCOME

VOLUME 1

SPECIAL EDIT

UPDATE

Becoming a CONTENT CREATOR

AND GROW YOUR BRAND

KEISHA L. HUNTER

You can get a copy by visiting:
https://pay.beautyprofitcoaching.com/f6b95cac-0fc7-4db3-a03a-6f0

Dedication

To my only daughter, Desiree. I became your mom at the age of 16. I fell in love with you instantly when the nurse told me I was pregnant. I was 15, and I had no clue how I was going to take care of you. Parenting is more than financial. I understand now that there was a lot I didn't have. But what I did know without any hesitation, without even understanding what I was about to experience, I was willing to go through whatever sacrifice I had to in order to make sure you had everything you needed. I didn't do everything right. I was a kid learning and teaching another kid who happens to be my daughter. We both were learning. Some things we learned together, and some things I already knew before you were even born.

I'm your mother! I'm not perfect by any means, nor do I carry any kind of guilt when it comes to me as a mother or a woman. I sacrificed my life for you. I wanted you, without even knowing what to do. I love you, and I pray that God will allow you to forgive me for those moments that were special to you, and I couldn't be there because I was working, trying to provide for us. I'm sorry, and I thought I was making the best decision to have myself financially in a good spot so that

I could at least afford and allow you opportunities that I did not have. I was a single parent with no assistance. Your dad wasn't there financially, emotionally, or mentally. I did the best I knew, and I thank God daily because it could've been worse.

You didn't become a teen mom like me. We did a pinky promise that you would let me know when you were ready for sex. You kept your promise and came and had a talk at 19. You graduated from high school and then went to college. I remember your junior prom. I was more excited than you. This was our first prom. I didn't get this experience. You shared it with me because you knew I had never had it. You chose your own dress, then from there, you allowed me to be as creative as I wanted. You were absolutely gorgeous. You looked just like a princess. You really didn't care, but I did, and I wanted you to have the best of the best. And that day was perfect. Now, at the age of 31, you decided to become a cosmetologist, not because of me but because you fell in love with it, and God made a decision to send you back to your mom so you could become equipped and ready to take on the industry called Cosmetology. Nobody can do it like God. Some things have to be in order to become!

I love you, your mom.

This dedication is to my late grandmother, Martha Hunter. She lived with my mom and me, so I was always surrounded by her wisdom. She was also a strong lady. Being an only child, my grandmother was the person I could talk to and ask anything, and she would answer it to the best of her ability. I remember when I was 19 and she cosigned for me to get a brand new car. My mom tried to talk her out of it. She didn't think I was mature enough or responsible enough to maintain a car. My first car was a '89 Toyota Corolla. As a matter of fact, Carl, my stepfather, cosigned for that car. When I was about 18, the car was wrecked, and I didn't like it anymore. I had my eyes on the Mazda 626. I eventually traded in the Toyota, and my grandmother signed the papers for me. Her words were, "I don't have to worry about Keisha. She's gonna be all right," and she signed that paper without any hesitation.

She lived to be 90. She got a chance to meet my daughter and watch her grow up all the way through her freshman year of college. I could hear her now telling me, "Keisha, I don't have to worry about you." That was my confirmation that she was proud.

I called her mama, not grandma, and if she could see me now, she would be proud. Thank you, Mama, for all those pep talks. Thank you for allowing me to be the inquisitive little girl that I was. I was always interested and always curious, and I asked a lot of questions. Mama would answer them all, but my mother felt like my grandma would let me get away with too much. As I write this, I think about my mother and my daughter. I think she lets her get away with too much, but there's one thing my grandmother taught me, and that is some people need more than others.

That response came from me asking her about what we call favoritism. I had two older cousins, and even though my grandmother lived with me, it sometimes felt like they were her favorites, and because I was curious and inquisitive, I asked her about what I saw as a kid, and her response was right. There were some things they needed from her, and that was her position, because there was nothing I could ask of her and she didn't do. She taught me a lesson on that day, and I was just a little girl, but I still remember it today. Everything you see is not real. You gotta ask questions. Thank you, Mama. I love you, and I know you're smiling down on me. I'm so glad that you were able to see me make my dreams a reality! She even told me I was gonna be the one to prepare her to go be with the Father. I was just a kid dreaming of becoming a hairstylist. She said you're gonna fix me up, and I remember telling her, "No, I'm going with you." She would laugh. Well, I followed her instructions. I prepared her for her Homegoing! I did it, Mama, just like you said I would.

Rest in Heaven,

Rest in Doggy Heaven, to my two Fur Babies

Fluffy & Gracie.

I MISS Y'ALL GIRLS SO MUCH!

2025 came in like a bang. I had lost both of y'all. Fluffy was 17. She had to be put down, which was a very hard decision. I cried like a baby, as did my daughter. I bought her for my daughter's 15th birthday. She wanted a dog. I kept Fluffy when she went off to college. That's how I ended up falling in love with her. Then, about 45 days later, Gracie died of dog depression. I was so sad, I had never imagined life without them. They were my girls. But God had a different plan. As I'm writing, one has been gone for seven months, and the other for eight months. I have my moments where I miss their presence, rushing home to them, meeting me at the door. My pit bull, Gracie, thought she was a little like Fluffy, who was a Pomeranian. I know, everybody asks how in the world they got along. They were inseparable. Fluffy was the oldest, and Gracie was the baby. They were a mess, too!

I miss my girls.

I WANT TO THANK ALL MY CLIENTS WHO HAVE RODE WITH ME THROUGH MY JOURNEY OF ENTREPRENEURSHIP. I STARTED WITH NO CLIENTS TWO DECADES AGO, WITH NO EXPERIENCE, JUST A DREAM. I THANK THOSE WHO STAYED. I THANK THOSE WHO HAVE LEFT TOO. EVERY ONE OF YOU GAVE ME AN OPPORTUNITY TO PROVIDE MY EXPERIENCE TO YOU, AND FOR THAT, I'M TRULY GRATEFUL. WITHOUT IT, I WOULD NOT HAVE BEEN ABLE TO HAVE SUSTAINED THIS LONG. I'VE BEEN BLESSED TO SERVE SOME EXTRAORDINARY WOMEN. WE'VE LAUGHED UNTIL OUR JAWS HURT. SOME I'VE LEARNED FROM, SOME I'VE CRIED WITH, SOME I'VE PRAYED WITH. THEY ALL KNOW ONE THING ABOUT KEISHA—YOU'RE GONNA LEAVE FEELING BETTER THAN HOW YOU CAME IN.

IT STARTS FROM THE INSIDE, THEN IT BEGINS TO SHOW ON THE OUTSIDE. THE HAIR IS JUST THE CHERRY ON TOP!

THANK Y'ALL SO MUCH FOR TRUSTING ME. I CANNOT SHOWCASE THIS GIFT CALLED COSMETOLOGY WITHOUT YOU.

Contents

Foreword — 1

Introduction — 5

Chapter 1: Hard Work Pays Off — 11

Chapter 2: Stick To Your Goals — 19

Chapter 3: Encourage Yourself — 27

Chapter 4: Know When To Hold And Fold — 31

Chapter 5: I'm Still Standing — 35

Chapter 6: After The Climb — 39

Chapter 7: Who Do You Think You Are? — 43

Acknowledgments — 47

Read More! — 51

About The Author — 55

Urgent Plea! — 57

Foreword

Let me start by saying, I didn't care much for Keisha. I guess it was the way that she was introduced to me. I already had friends, and, bam, here we go, Keisha Hunter. Thinking back, I was the alpha of my group, and I knew that she was an alpha as well from her personality. I didn't know how it was gonna work. It didn't take long before we became the best of friends. It was the first day of ninth grade, and she was sort of reserved because she was at a new school. She was laid back but very outspoken. I realized that she would fit in the group perfectly.

I always felt like I had to protect her since she was the smallest of the bunch, but I quickly realized she could hold her own. She didn't need me as much as I thought she did. I watched her become a teenage mother (single mother at that), and she was a child herself. I can honestly say this was the only time I ever felt jealousy of her. I wanted a baby, too. I wanted us to do it together. Anyway, Keisha had to become an adult, and it wasn't easy. She had no high school education and a baby, and she was just barely old enough to work, but she had to do what she had to do. She had left home and worked several jobs. It was hard, and I hate that I wasn't a good friend to her at this time. I was battling my own mess, but I always knew our friendship was solid.

I love that woman with all my heart. That's my Bookie. We created that name for us 30 years ago, and she's still my bookie today! Over the years, she grew up and did some things to better herself. She needed to make sure her daughter was fed and had a roof over her head.

I am glad to say Keisha worked hard. She started her own business, and she helped people with jobs. She even helped me get myself back on track by giving me a job responsible for all the money that came through her business, considering I was in transition of turning my life around. She didn't know if I was capable or not, but she trusted me, and I didn't want to let her down or myself. This was my opportunity to prove I was a changed person. I was her receptionist for about five years.

Keisha never gave up on me. I remember she forced me to get my license. I had been driving illegally for years, but I was trying to do things right. Not long after getting my license, Keisha had a car ready for me. It needed some work, but I could drive it. It was a Money Green Honda Accord, but it worked until I was able to better myself, and I did. She was the one who convinced me I could be independent and try for my own place. I did, and I've been going ever since.

I love that woman with all my heart. She's gonna push you into your greatness. You're not gonna like it. Her delivery can be tough, but it's all in love, and she sees potential and is willing to work with you if you are trying. She's not a pushover. Her small frame delivers like a giant. If you ever have an opportunity to meet her, take advantage of the opportunity. She's a rare gem full of experience. That's my Bookie! And throughout all this, people still didn't like her, and when I asked her what it was that people just didn't like, she told me, "I won't let them control me." I didn't understand, but I know now that it's her spirit. Keisha is a good person with a good heart, but it takes a certain kind of person to understand it.

You see, special people attract special people, and I'm glad that the good Lord put us together. I understand her, and she understands me. Sometimes we just look at each other and we know what the other is thinking. It's funny because the haters wish they had that. People have been jealous of our friendship since we were kids. We are damn near 50, and we still run into those types of people who have never had or experienced what true friendship is. I tell her all the time, it's gonna be us till the end. Anybody who missed out is missing out on a very, very special lady. I don't say this because she's my friend. It's because I've messed up before. I said in the beginning I wasn't always there, but let me tell you something, there has never been a time when this lady was not there for me. I can call her anytime, and she's gonna respond. Thank you for seeing me through my mess. I can't wait until she gets everything in life she deserves and wants. I love her and always will ... 30 years plus y'all keep watching cause we are growing old together ... Love you, Bookie!

Introduction

Growing up as an only child, I always felt different. I was even told quite frequently that I was wise for my age. I was just a kid, so I had no idea what that meant. I didn't know what it was or even understand its favor until I grew up. I never felt accepted by my peers. Growing up, I always seemed to end up around older people. My mom didn't like it nor approve because she felt they were too advanced for me. I felt like I was learning what to do and what not to do. I didn't have any siblings in the home. I did learn as I got older that my dad had more kids. That's another book by itself.

Anyway, I didn't have a model. They were my models, and it kept me out of a lot of trouble. I was a very inquisitive kid, and I grew up with my mom, who was the baby of 11. They come from a small country town located in North Carolina. My mom was a single parent, and she did the best she could, but I was a kid who had big dreams, and my big dreams scared the hell out of my mom. I remember telling her as a kid that I was going to be very successful. I was going to live in a big house, and I was going to drive a BMW. She looked at me as if she was thinking, "How do you think you are going to achieve these things?" At that time, we lived in a small apartment that was located in a rough neighborhood. We never lived in what they called the projects, but we always lived in rough neighborhoods.

At that time, I didn't realize they were rough. I do remember seeing drug activities and prostitution. I heard gunshots every night. I just assumed that was normal. I didn't always like the places, but I thought the neighborhood was fun. I always found some older girls to hang out with. My mom eventually bought her first home when I was 14, so she made a decision to get me out of those neighborhoods before she felt like it got too bad.

It was a process. I had grown used to what I was seeing and hearing daily, and the new neighborhood where she purchased her home was boring. Too quiet with nobody hanging out and nobody walking up and down the street. I didn't like it. I was not used to that. I always tell people I had one foot on the good side and one foot on the bad side. Even though I was a dreamer, my environment was fun. The majority of the time, we don't understand as kids what our parents are doing, but if you see evidence that's showing you they want more and better for you, then that's what it is. I rebelled against what my mom was trying to do, even though we were in this new middle-class neighborhood. My thought process was stuck in the old neighborhood. I even had my mom go to the school board to go to a different high school prior to moving because I thought I was going to be different.

INTRODUCTION

I was getting prepared for my new beginnings, so I thought I would end up meeting some girls at the new school who were middle-class girls, but they were rebellious like me, so even though I was in a new neighborhood and a new school, I did not have a new mindset. I did not have a new thought process. You have to change your thinking to make any kind of changes in your life. You will not change anything with the same thinking. Life has a way of showing you that you will have to make some changes, or you can suffer the consequences of your actions. Those are the two options. Some of us get tired of suffering and make a decision that we want to change our lives; therefore, we have to change our thinking.

I was what you called hard-headed, just rebellious. You say right, I'm going left. I didn't believe the fire would burn until I was in the fire, so I was one of the ones who learned from their experience and suffered the consequences of my actions here. I was a kid thinking I was the smartest one in the room, a kid with no experience, yet I knew so much, so I thought. I'm so grateful to God for not allowing me to go through worse. It could have been worse. My actions eventually landed me in a big fire that forced me to become the person that I had dreamed of so many times as a kid.

I remember hearing things like, "Don't bite off more than you can chew," and "What's done in the dark always comes to the light." "If you make your bed hard, you lie in it." I think this was the hardest one. I knew every roadblock I was dealing with I had created myself. I could not blame anyone but me. I think that's why accountability is so important to me. I believe when you make a conscious decision to react, you cannot later blame someone else for the repercussions of your actions. It's your responsibility. In the same way you were able to confidently make a decision, you have to be the same with the outcome and consequences. You don't get to choose the consequences when you make decisions to stand boldly. Then you have to understand that not everybody is going to agree with you.

We all know we are not gonna please everyone, but I must say there have been a few that let me know my work has not been in vain—thank you! You all know who you are! Now let's help those like we all needed it! Stay Hungry. And focus. Stay grounded. Your commitment and consistency will pay off! I experienced a lot of setbacks and a lot of roadblocks, but I did not give up. I wanted to. There has to be a light in you that shines even when you're dark. That light is your reminder of why you started. This is not the same light to let you know you're getting closer to the end. The end light is brighter. You can actually see what you are trying to do. The light of doubt is dim. You can't see yourself. I had to learn that I was allowing doubt to creep in. I was responsible for my thoughts, and I determined my happiness. No one else can make you happy. I thank God for my climb. I learned how to fight not physically, but emotionally and mentally, for what makes me happy.

It took some time to embrace my differences. I remember hearing people say I did not ask God for this; He gave it to me. I had to learn to embrace the gifts and talents He gave me. I can truly say I'm learning to embrace every gift and talent that God has given me. I'm sorry to those who are offended, but I'm going to use it to help as many people as I can. That's the goal. My life was not this hard for me not to be an example to show you what the light looks like at the end of the tunnel. It gets better afterward. We tend to think all the good stuff is at the beginning, and yeah, it is fun. I had a ball climbing, but I also had to learn through all adversities and setbacks. I don't have any doubts now about who God says I am. I learned so much about myself—who I am and who I'm becoming. I remember when my grandmother used to say to just live a little bit longer. She was right. It's the after climb.

I'm finally here.

This walk called life can and will be lonely sometimes for you. Being an only child and the first business owner had its challenges. You don't have a model, so everything you're doing is from scratch. God is your only source. Without God, I don't know where I would be today, and I say that because you may be the first person in your family to go to college or to finish high school. You may be the first of something, and you are going to feel alone, and it's OK. Again, you have to know your purpose and know that this is what you are supposed to be doing. Otherwise, you will be distracted and discouraged because you are the first. Make sure you are doing everything to stay strong to build your strength through prayer and meditation, so that when you have to defend, you know how to fight. Yes, you will get knocked down sometimes, but through every adversity, you get stronger and wiser, and you learn how to keep going and not give up. The climb is not easy, but it will be worth it. I know now that I can be anything I want to be through hard work, determination, and perseverance. Just because you mess up along the way does not mean you can't fix it. The sky's the limit. Are you ready to climb? Let's go !! Let's go get what belongs to you. I will see you after the climb!

WHO DO YOU THINK YOU ARE?

CHAPTER 1

HARD WORK PAYS OFF

TRUST THE PROCESS!!

"If you believe, you can achieve" is a quote I often remind myself of. After getting pregnant at 15, I knew I had a long, hard road ahead of me. I remember telling my mom I was gonna fix it. I didn't know how it was gonna be done, but somehow, I knew it would. I gave birth to my daughter two months after my 16th birthday. I dropped out of high school because the government said my mom made enough money to financially support me and my unborn child at that time. Can you believe that? It got real!

This was not a dream. I had to tap into survival. This was sink or swim, and I had to learn how to swim quickly. When I think about it now, I'm grateful for my climb. My mom had just purchased her first home. And here I was pregnant. I didn't find out until later that my mom went through a period of depression because of my pregnancy. I'm her only child, so I can definitely understand her feelings now that I'm a mom. She was ashamed. She felt this was an impression on her parenting, and it wasn't. This was the repercussion of my actions. I knew I had disappointed my mom. It took her some time to acknowledge what was happening. I was about six months pregnant when I finally heard her say, "I'm ready for my grandbaby." She was trying to accept and embrace what I had done to myself, and she did.

She loves her granddaughter. I got my first job at McDonald's. I was about five months pregnant when I started that job. I stayed there until my daughter was about three months old. I eventually left there and started serving college students at a dining hall. I was about 17 years old, serving college students lunch. I was not feeling that job at all, but I did what I had to do to support my daughter. I was determined not to become a burden to my mom, especially since I was responsible for getting myself into this situation.

By the age of 18, I was a CNA (certified nursing assistant). One of my good girlfriends, still to this day, figured it was a good idea since it would guarantee me some steady income. My daughter was around one or two years old at this time. That wasn't my niche either. Even though I was getting a check, it wasn't what my heart desired. I wasn't feeling fulfilled at all, but I still trusted the process of staying consistent with work and paying my bills. I had rent and a car payment, plus I had my daughter to financially support. I don't know how I did it all. I know God is good.

When I was 19 years old, I started working in mental health. I started in group homes, and eventually, I started working with just one client, so that CNA certification came in handy. It wasn't mandatory, but it looked good on paper. I had finally landed something I felt good about, something I could stay in until my process started. I loved motivating and encouraging, so this was perfect. I worked in that field until I was about 21.

Even during that time, there was always a pull on me for more. I loved hair (cosmetology). I just didn't know how it was going to happen. I had so many other obstacles and roadblocks that I knew were gonna make things more challenging for me. I did not know how my life was going to turn out. At that present moment, I was a single mom with no diploma. But I kept dreaming, so I focused on what I had going on, which was my job and my own place. Yes, I had my first apartment too. I was about 18, and my daughter was about two years old. My mom and stepfather got married, and I was able to maintain his old apartment. I was working, so I was able to pay the bills. I didn't do everything right because it was my first place, so of course, I didn't know everything that I was doing, but I did manage to live there for five years until I went to beauty school.

I was about 19 when I decided to go back to school for my GED. It was gonna allow me to finish early. Trying to get my remaining high school credits was gonna take longer. Remember, I was pregnant during my sophomore year of high school, and I didn't have a lot of credits. After graduating from my local community college at 20, I obtained my GED. I had to take five different tests, composed of all the curriculum you would get in high school. Similar to a crash course, I had to have five different books to be able to study. I couldn't afford them, so you know what I did? I took all five. I know, in your mind, you think, "She stole those books." I did. I needed them so badly. I asked God to forgive me, and I know He knew if I could have afforded to purchase them, I would have.

I didn't have the money. I did have determination. Not long afterwards, I enrolled and graduated from beauty school. As a little girl, I knew this was what I wanted to do. I knew this was my passion. I was finally there. I was ready for my new beginnings. I was so proud of myself for working hard and trusting the process. I couldn't believe I did it! All the crying, praying, and sacrifice had finally paid off.

I was finally a licensed cosmetologist. I didn't want to let myself down or my daughter, who was gonna one day grow up. I wanted her to know that it's not how you start, it's about how you finish. It's about you being determined and resilient. I was very determined not to allow society to tell me that because I was a teen mom, my daughter would more than likely not be successful. I was already dealing with the name-calling of being a fast ass and being too grown. Yes, I felt ashamed. I was 15 and pregnant. Now that I'm older, I can recall those feelings. But God! Well, we fooled them and broke all those odds. You already know, we shut their mouths up.

My daughter graduated from high school. She went to college. I never went to college, and none of those people who called me names did either. She did, and now she's a licensed cosmetologist as well. You can't beat a determined person.

Good things come to those who are patient and work hard, and I have done both. I was building character and didn't know it yet. I was just working, going to school, trying to correct my wrongs, and trying to get my life back on track. I was trying to be a good role model for my daughter. I wanted her to not only believe but know with boldness and confidence that she makes all her dreams come true.

Don't ask me how I knew what to do or even say to her. I didn't, but I believed, and I was bold and confident enough to try! I was her model for those life lessons I was teaching her. She was my reason why I had to try. She was watching me. I never wanted her to feel that I was expecting more from her than I was willing to do. I remember I used to tell my mom, you don't know until you try. She would just look at me. She played things a little safer than I did, but I can appreciate the distinction, and she did damn well for her and her husband. They are the lenders and not the borrowers. They both are retired, living life like it's golden. They broke the curse of working for bills. They are living debt-free. After the climb.

You don't realize it yet, but you are not only working on goals. You are working on yourself as well. Indirectly, you are forming habits, good or bad, and you get to decide what their benefits will be. Growth requires sacrifice that most people are not willing to make. It requires you to be able to see ahead, rather than what's happening now. If you can't see it, then you probably are not gonna make the necessary sacrifices to accomplish your goals. You have to be so determined and sick and tired of your present situation that frustration should ignite your fire to fight for what you want and what you see.

I gave up my first apartment and moved back with my parents, sharing a room and a bed with my seven-year-old daughter at the time. This was the sacrifice for my dreams to come true. This was a tough sacrifice. Sleeping in the bed with my daughter probably was hard for her too; she had never shared her bed with anyone. She was two when we moved out. By now, I had been on my own for about five years, and moving back in with your parents can be challenging. We all know they have rules. In my mind, I was grown. I made it through and eventually moved back into my own place. Sacrifice is about giving up things that you love and really want. I love freedom. I guess that's why I'm an entrepreneur. I also gave up my part-time job so I could go to school at night. I worked full-time during the day. School was 17 months part-time. Trusting the process was not easy, but I knew I wanted to be a full-time hairstylist. I no longer wanted to do just any job.

This is where behavior meets character. Character produces integrity. Integrity produces discipline, and you're gonna need a lot of discipline to trust the process.

The definition of integrity is the quality of being honest and having strong moral principles and moral uprightness. Most people think what's done in the dark stays in the dark. Wrong! It's actually who you are when no one is around. The person you are when you are alone is the real person, just you and your thoughts. We tend to think it's all about the action and not the perception. Perception is all about awareness.

Action is doing, and just because you are doing something doesn't mean you really want to. Sometimes, we do things because we have to. So don't believe the hype with actions. Yes, they can speak louder than words, but the perception is where we find your true belief system. How you perceive yourself will be the outcome. If you think you can't, you won't. If you think you can, then there will be no limitations on who or what you think you can do. Your thoughts determine your life. Your brain is like a computer. What you download will produce, so it's very important that you constantly reevaluate your thoughts.

Stay positive. Everything changes. Nothing stays the same. Sometimes, you have to upgrade your computer. Your thoughts are the same; otherwise, you will react and even respond more slowly than you would if you don't do self-evaluation. Again, if computers run slowly, usually there's a virus. You can't skip the hard work; here is where you build character, integrity, confidence, tenacity, resilience, endurance, discipline, and courage. All ingredients are needed for the climb. It's just like following a recipe. You can't skip any steps. You can add steps. If you stop in the middle of your process with doubt or fear, you will slow your process down with distractions of not trusting the work you put in. Don't worry about the end. The end is when you stop keeping your focus on what's happening now and what's important right now . Unless you are willing to trust the process, you won't get to the destination that's aligned for you. There is always something new on the other side.

You must be willing to make sacrifices to achieve success. Sacrifices most people are not willing to make. I was willing. I wanted to see. Ask yourself, will you do anything to be successful? Are you willing to give up the things you love now for better options later? Sacrificing is giving up the things you really love and don't want to give up. It takes certain types of people to do it. Are you one? You have to believe and be able to see what you believe and believe you are capable of making it come true. Sounds like pressure, right? No worries, it's only pressure when you are not aligned. Now, don't get me wrong, you will get nervous, butterflies, and all the feelings you get from working. We all know when we haven't worked for something and it was given to us without any grace or gratitude, God gives gifts, too. They flow naturally, so don't get them confused. There is a difference. You don't put in the same type of commitment for some reason I don't know, but when we actually put in some work, you are more grateful and appreciative in gaining an understanding of sticking to your goals and executing the plan.

How bad do you want it?

CHAPTER 2

STICK TO YOUR GOALS

EXECUTE THE PLAN

So far, you have learned what can happen if you stick to your goals and trust the process. This process is not an easy process, especially depending on where you are starting from, beginning, middle, or end. Generally, you are so excited at the beginning, working hard, doing whatever needs to be done, until you see what you believe by the middle. You start straddling the fence, questioning if it's ever gonna happen for you. You become doubtful, and you barely believe it yourself. By the end, you are so close to giving up and throwing in the towel that you don't see anything. Now, you are at the point of stopping what you started. You are so close to making your goals a reality. I know when you hear it's closer than you think that it sounds cliché, but it's real. It's the truth. You are very close. You can do it! Stay consistent, and results will come.

Your job is to do the work, have faith, and continue executing your plan until you are living what you said you wanted to see.

At 23, I was self-employed, and I managed to stick to my goals. Life finally seemed like it was lining up. You don't think about it, but each new beginning is exactly what it says it is; you have to start from ground zero. This is not a place everybody is willing to go to. Here, I was fighting again for my life. At least that's how it feels each time you attempt to climb. You have to start from the beginning. This time, not only was I trying to build myself a business that needed clients, but this was my only source of income to provide for my daughter and myself. Like I said in Chapter 1, if you believe you can achieve, that means you have to believe that you see yourself at the place you want to be. If you cannot see it, you will not reach for it. If you don't believe it, you will not achieve it.

Well, I didn't just talk. I was a woman of my word. If I said I was gonna do it, trust me, it was gonna happen. I couldn't always tell you when, but I just knew it would. I didn't always know the processes I would have to go through, and to be honest, if you knew the process, you probably wouldn't even go through it. Yes, it was hard. I had left both jobs, one for school and the other to follow my dreams. I had my mom, who didn't understand. She wanted me to go work at a real job. I struggled to make ends meet. I remember asking God, "Did I do the right thing, and if I did, why am I struggling?"

I hadn't struggled like this since my daughter was a baby. By this point, she was maybe 9. What I didn't realize at the time was that I was building strength and resilience and learning a new beginning. Sometimes, when we go too fast, we miss the lesson. I know we want it now, but the flip side is, do you want to get to your desired place and not be equipped to handle it? Not being prepared? The lesson is where the growth takes place and the maturity in understanding alignment and the assignment. Think about driving without any training. How hectic would that be, right? The training builds your confidence, and the more you drive, the more experienced you become.

I continued to trust the process of showing up, wishing, and praying for my clientele to one day be like some of the ladies I was watching and admiring. I was still responsible for paying booth rent even though I didn't have clients. Entrepreneurs have to put money out first with the hope and prayer of a return or profit. Not everybody is built for it. I remember daydreaming about my turn and what I was gonna do when it came around. I started preparing for what I wanted by enhancing my skills, taking classes, going to shows, and getting certifications under my belt so that when that time came, I would be ready.

They say if you stay ready, you won't have to get ready, so that's what I started doing, positioning myself around the right people, places, and things and staying consistent. Before I knew it, I was five years in the game. By the age of 28/29 years old, my dedication and hard work had gotten my clientele up to around 50 women a week. I was officially a 6-figure stylist. I was finally where I wanted to be. I finally felt like I was making some noise, as we used to say. I finally felt like my work was speaking. I was doing the damn thing! I was trained to go. I always worked for everything, no easy passes over here.

After accomplishing my goals, I was ready to show other people how I had built my business. I had dreamed of owning my own salon, but there was this doubt: even though I'm a dreamer, I still feel all the feelings. I get nervous. I get scared. The difference is I still try even though I am scared, and there's a lesson in pushing yourself through. Keep going. I knew I couldn't afford to start a business financially, or even had the resources to do so, which was my thinking. However, little did I know, my blessing was being prepared for me. I just had to keep going through my process.

God has a blessing with your name on it! Believe it. There was always this voice saying, "Don't push it, now you've got your cosmetologist license, be satisfied. You made more money than you dreamed of at this point. Who do you think you are?" But there was this stigma with hairstylists about us not being able to work together and being unprofessional. I wanted to change that narrative. I had been renting a booth for about eight years. By this time, I was given my salon. You read it right! God did it! He had a salon being prepared for me. My turn was finally there. I was given a salon fully furnished, ready to go. All the things I was concerned about not having, I never needed any of them. All I had to do was walk through the door. That's how God does it.

Smooth sailing is my motto. I had to build my team while I worked. They had done all the cosmetic building; now it was time for me to execute my plan. I didn't know the salon was being renovated. It was right across the hall from the barbershop/salon I was working in. How convenient was that? Remember when I said if you stay ready, you won't have to get ready? Unfortunately, we don't get to determine the time; our job is to get in position for our opportunity because it will come. And when it does, you will either rise to the occasion or miss the opportunity.

I started creating marketing material to let the stylist know we had a new salon in town through the mail. I would do interviews in between my clients while I worked. I had seven chairs, and we had a receptionist who handled the appointments and checked the clients out. My salon was located in the mall in Durham, NC. We grossed over two hundred thousand in our first ten months in business. This was obviously bigger than me. I was aligned. My first time in business, I had never managed anyone outside myself. Somehow, through the grace of God, He allowed me to use my common sense. Treating people the way I wanted was the most important piece to me. Are you gonna make everyone happy? No, my job was to be at peace and not make it personal when it comes to making the best decisions for the business and the staff.

Over the years, I had experienced some tough situations renting a booth. One lady abruptly moved; the other went through a name change. I had to rebuild my clients both times. Neither time was I aware of what was about to happen. I was still new in the industry and had already been through some unstable situations. This was my income; my career was being uprooted because of someone else's mess. I can handle my own mess. Those two incidents taught me that I wanted to be more in control of my career. Even though you are considered self-employed, you are not the business owner, and that's who makes the decisions. I knew I had experienced some disruptions that weren't because of me, and I was not gonna do that to people. I was willing to do the work so that I could create a unified team. I didn't want to be just a salon; I wanted us to be known as professionals. We were in uniform and on one accord.

My vision was to provide an experience for the customer, not just a service. We were a seven-chair commission salon open seven days a week. As the owner, the business supplied all products and was financially responsible for all daily operations. In turn, my profit was 60% per chair. We had our own commercial where our local cable network came to the salon to shoot for us, which generated a lot of business from that marketing. In business, you are not gonna satisfy everybody. Some people are never gonna acknowledge how you've helped them, and that's ok. You know, and that's all that matters. Everybody is not gonna pat you on the back, and if you are doing it for a pat, you need to go evaluate why you are doing it again.

Stay true to yourself and your abilities. Distractions tend to show up when you are doing good, they say … Success doesn't come by mistreating or manipulating. You have to take the designated lane that's aligned for you to take. That lane will have everything you need, whether you are learning or teaching. That lane will have what you need for your assignment and lesson. You won't know until you execute your plan! You will have to learn to encourage yourself and pat your own back. What sacrifices are you willing to make for your goals? How disciplined are you without supervision? Are you trustworthy? You will have to be willing to cheer yourself on. Learn how to encourage yourself even when no one is patting you on the back.

Remember, this is what you wanted. You must be able to stand alone or be persuaded by others; it's up to you! The majority of the time, the people who have the most to say have never even tried to do what you were doing, but they can tell you what you should and should not be doing. Again, don't be persuaded. This is your vision, and as long as you are being authentically yourself, you are doing the right thing. Pat yourself on the back for staying true to you!

CHAPTER 3

ENCOURAGE YOURSELF

PAT YOURSELF ON THE BACK

Be your own cheerleader. As you start working on your goals, not everyone is gonna be happy or agree with everything you see or say. It's not their responsibility to support you. I learned early that you cannot take business personally. You cannot wear your heart on your sleeve. If you are looking for confirmation to do whatever it is you need to do for yourself, you won't ever complete what needs to be done. There will even be times your family and friends will doubt you. You have to be so confident in what you see that you are willing to go through the process alone. I remember when I was in the transition of leaving my full-time job. Everybody thought I had lost my mind. They reminded me that I had a child. What they didn't understand was that I was doing it for my child. I had already made things hard for myself. I at least wanted to have myself in a position that I felt good about through my accomplishments to be able to financially support myself and my daughter.

I was the first entrepreneur in the family, breaking traditions of working a 9-5 job, which too has its own disadvantages. You are the first, right? You will find yourself typically misunderstood. Who do you think you are? What makes you so different from the rest of us? I was asked a few times if I was just trying to fulfill my goals. I didn't feel like I was better than anybody, family friends, nobody, but they were my examples of what I didn't want, which was a 9-5. I love my freedom, and I did not like having to ask if I could have days off when I needed them off. I knew early on through my dreaming that I'm a leader.

It's very important that you are confident in what you believe; otherwise, you will be easily persuaded from your climb. People want to stay and keep you in their comfort zones. Not yours, nothing grows there. You are just in routine if you notice some people get very upset when you take them out of their routine. It's because they are entering something unfamiliar. Anxiety and fear kick in because you don't have any information. That's why it's a journey. You don't know. You have to follow your heart. That's where true happiness and peace come from.

Most people are afraid to try, not understanding that you learn something you didn't know before. If you don't step out and try something new, you will not create new memories and experiences. When you believe, you can achieve! I always told myself that, as I was climbing, even in those tough times, I would sometimes question the process due to it seeming unreachable. And I definitely had a lot of those moments. After all, I was the first entrepreneur. I didn't have anyone in my family who understood where I was in my life.

I would encourage you to get a prayer life. If it wasn't for my spirituality, I don't know where I would be. Trusting the process is not easy. Most people don't understand the sacrifices that you make or are willing to make. Don't lose focus, and don't get caught up in the money chase. It's so easy to do. The more you get, the more you want. Stay true to you, then you will eventually begin to see it's all part of the process. Don't be so hard on yourself. You are still standing through it all. You've learned how not to lose your drive and determination to win, and you are becoming a better person. That eventually gets you closer to your purpose. Be your own cheerleader. As you start working on your goals, not everyone is gonna be happy or agree with everything you see or say. Eventually, the climb gets clearer. You begin to understand that being true means losing some people whom you may love or care about. It doesn't mean you are better than them by trying to accomplish your goal. It proves that your company can push you up or pull you down.

At some point, you have to decide what's more important to you. The majority of the time, these are not even the people who encourage you, and you are worried about what they are gonna say or think. If they are real, they are gonna hold you and push you all the way. Those that fall off were supposed to. Sometimes it's your family, your blood. This is where it gets tricky because they are your blood. You love them, and it can become challenging when you have to make decisions about your life. If you're not careful, they will make you feel like you're not supposed to be climbing, when the reality is, they should be climbing too. When you are being authentically yourself, you learn that you can stand alone until the right people show up.

Family is not always through blood. I remember the saying blood is thicker than water. This is not necessarily true. We have some family members who can create chaos and then play victim. Be aware and be conscious that this can pull on your heart. They are human and capable of doing things to prevent your climb. The risk becomes too great to just get attached to anyone. This is a season where you learn to be quiet and trust the plan. This is a season you will have to encourage yourself as you begin achieving your goals. This requires you to do some things differently. You will have to make some changes to yourself as a person. And a lot of the time, this is where you can separate the doers and talkers.

Staying consistent can be challenging. It can be even more challenging at times when you have to do it alone. These are the times when I used to ask myself, "How bad do I want it?" I wanted it badly. I was willing to leave the old to see what the new had for me. Do it scared. You will amaze yourself, and the stronger you become in your new life, the more confident you become in who you are becoming. You've got this!

CHAPTER 4

KNOW WHEN TO HOLD AND FOLD

IT'S OK TO THROW IN THE TOWEL

So far, we have learned that hard work pays off. Stick to your goals, trust your process, and encourage yourself. In this chapter, we will learn when to hold and when to fold. Even as an entrepreneur, you must know when to throw in the towel. Each person's limits will be different. The reasoning will be the same, whether it is not getting results or being unfulfilled. For either one, you will need to evaluate the situation to determine whether to hold or fold. Neither one is gonna be easier than the other, considering we've been working on the steps. The goal is to get you to your place of purpose.

In 2016, I built a full cosmetic art school from the ground up. It takes two years to get accredited. In that process, you are financially responsible for any and everything that's needed to operate as a school. I had to have a kit and books in advance for the students. They needed an instructor whom I had to pay, plus the bills to keep the doors open. We stayed open almost five years and graduated some students, nowhere close to the vision I had, which was to educate the students, then hire them in the salon to work.

That project almost took me out mentally, emotionally, and definitely financially. I had not learned yet when to fold, so I held on. And the more I held on, the heavier it became. I was determined it was gonna be what I saw, thinking that because I had dotted all the lines, done my homework, and had gone through all the steps, it would work. The reason why it wasn't working was that I was doing it wrong. I was taking all the questions I had personally. I even questioned myself. "What made me think I could do this anyway?" Life was finally showing me I was not in control and that there is a God. And just because you want something doesn't mean it's supposed to be.

That was a very dark season. Everything I knew was no longer, and I had to submit to the transition of life or continue fighting for a project that was not giving me the results I needed. I just couldn't accept that it was not happening the way I intended. I said the way I intended. That was a hard lesson to learn, thinking, because it's what I wanted, it was supposed to be. Life has a way of showing you, you ain't in control of nothing. So I made the decision to finally close the school.

I closed another salon I had opened to help financially foot the school, while my salon in the mall was able to operate without me. I had created a system through commission that just needed the stylist to operate to create their income. The salon I closed was in another city, so I packed my things up and left and never looked back. I came back home and started cleaning up this mess I had made through my actions of chasing money and wanting more money. I was already doing well. I knew I had heard God tell me to build the school. He did not tell me to chase the money. It was the intent that prevented it from becoming what I saw. I got caught up in the money. You could get up to $17,000 per student, and baby, I was trying to get it.

I had climbed so far up through my hard work, and it was time to throw in the towel. Most of the time, we think throwing in the towel means giving up. No, it means you have to know in your heart that you have done everything you can; once you've accomplished that, there you will find peace on when to hold and when to fold. As a little girl, my mom taught me to give one hundred percent in everything, no matter the outcome. The end result will be that you gave it everything you have, and that's all you can do. I can now say, unless you have the right support system and a prayer life, it's lonely at the top. It produces so much anxiety to stay in that spot.

As I started coming down the climb, it was hard. I was mad at God. I was mad at anyone and everyone who didn't help me. Then one day, I just got up, and I felt better. It was over. My desires of reaching and climbing and trying to become who I wanted to be. The pressure keeps you climbing; there is no end. As soon as you reach that one, you move on to the next one, and it keeps going. It was a total of three years in the wilderness. I made it through the storm. I'm still standing.

When you learn your achievements have nothing to do with the climb, you start realizing what's important. You start to see the value in your decisions and how important it is to be patient and not be in a rush for anything. Know that God has the perfect time set aside for you.

It reminds me of the quote, "He may not come when I want him, but He will always show up on time!" Every day, you get the opportunity to open your eyes that let you know you are still standing and that there is still a plan and purpose waiting for you. You weathered the storms of life. Pat yourself on the back for having the courage to go up the mountain top and then having the courage to come back down. Coming back down off the high ride can have its challenges, depending on the ride and how high up you get. That's why it's very important to have a relationship with our Heavenly Father, because if you don't, pain and disappointment can steal your identity. It can have you thinking you are a failure when, actually, you won when you made the decision to do something different. You will continue to go through ups and downs. You are now learning to adjust and not take life so personally. We have to be uncomfortable for growth, so when you are going through discomfort, know you are about to start something new. Don't be so hard on yourself. You've come a long way, and you are getting very close to the after climb. Don't give up. You're closer than you know. Your resilience is about to pay off!

CHAPTER 5

I'M STILL STANDING

I WEATHERED THE STORM

You stayed in the race, and now you are much lighter than before you started. With the pressure of life, give yourself grace and mercy. I weathered the storm. I survived it all: I can honestly say God allowed me to do everything I was big and bold enough to do. I understand when my grandma said, "You won't look like what you've been through." God is now using my story for his glory. I did everything I wanted, and through the grace of God, I'm still standing.

I remember when I bought my house. In 2011, I was abandoned by someone I loved and trusted. Three months into my purchase, he left me holding the bag. I was so scared. But God, here I was at 32 or 33 years old. I just purchased my first home in this prominent community on the golf course. I mean, literally, the golf course where I could see people playing golf. I didn't even choose this house. He loved it from the beginning. I eventually fell in love with it. It was a big house. It was just us, but hey, we were building businesses together. I definitely did not see this one coming. My mortgage was $2,200. I had never in my life paid that kind of money to live anywhere. I had been a business owner for a little over a year, and my daughter was off in college, so when I say me and God, I mean it.

This is where I learned that people will let you down. Even when they say, "I love you." I learned the difference between man and God. This was a learning season for me. I was sad no one knew. I was able to hide it, but when I was alone, that's when I was reminded of what I was going through. The pain I was in was my first adult relationship, and I got my heart broken, but I learned who I was as a person. I'm a survivor, and my faith is what has kept me. I could have lost my mind.

There were times I felt like I had to thank God for having my business and the staff with the responsibility. It kept me getting up every day. It kept me fighting. Without it, I don't know what could have happened. I also learned forgiveness. I had to forgive that person for hurting me and abandoning me in a situation I had never been in before. As I grew and matured, I realized that sometimes the people who love you can also hurt you, not always intentionally, even though it may feel like it. It's their lack of maturity that's allowing them to hurt you.

As you grow, you learn the true definition of empathy. You learn that if a person has shown and proven to you that they love you, then, more than likely, they hurt you out of fear.

Fear will make you scared of the unknown. You have to be able to distinguish the intent of a person. Hurt people do hurt people. And even though you may have compassion, it doesn't diminish the hurt it creates.

I remember asking my mom, "What am I gonna do?" Her exact words were, "You are gonna continue on and keep living your life." So I did., I picked myself up like I do, and I started rebuilding, learning to take life one day at a time and giving myself grace and mercy. I started learning that you really are not in control of anything. Enjoy the moment. When that one is over, there will be more opportunities waiting. We get so attached that we really think it's guaranteed. Nothing is but life and death. The only separation is that everyone doesn't live their life. Life is about living and creating experiences and memories by doing new things. Learn how to pick yourself back up and weather the storm so you can learn to stand through those experiences.

Adversity is how you develop confidence. Your confidence comes from you being willing to do things scared and to do it without anyone else cheering you on but you. You become a model for others who may be stuck between their climbs. Your resilience and strength will be a model, whether you are going up or coming back down. Both take courage and confidence. We get so caught up in winning that we forget there are lessons in not right now. It gives you an opportunity to gear up again. This time, you have more information and more confidence than you have ever had.

Congratulations! Now your job is to maintain and continue learning. If things didn't go as planned the first time, you get another chance. The next time, you are more prepared, fired up, and ready for your win. You, too, must continue the work to maintain the win! You made it this far. You obviously are doing some things right. Keep up the good work, continue checking you and your intentions, and you will get to the after-climb.

Your mind and thoughts are stable now. You no longer have to go through or feel like you're in a survival mode. Now that you are living, you have a better understanding that everything is already divine and aligned, and once you become aligned at the right time, you will become who you are supposed to be. We have gone through some tough adversities, but through it all, we can say, "I'm still standing." If you had to ask yourself, would you want more adversities or fewer? And which way do you learn more from doing, more or less? You can be anything you want with discipline and determination. You will WIN! Now, what you consider a win is up to you. You can do it. I'm cheering for you to get to your after-climb.

CHAPTER 6

AFTER THE CLIMB

The word "I" is now replaced with "God Did It!" I went before the climb, and I got a chance to live a life I never dreamed of. I reached what they called the top. I've lived in big houses, mansions, or whatever you call them. I had one on the golf course where I was harassed for even being able to afford it. I've driven the finest of the fine. I've eaten at the best restaurant where they made me feel like I was the only one in the room. I've experienced that my bank, which I had been with for five years, didn't learn my name until they felt like I had some money. They know by how much money you keep in the bank. It's marketing. You won't know this unless you reach this status, and again, it's a choice.

No position is better than the other. I showed you my parents in the beginning, who worked a 9-5, and their climb is also not what society says. We are all trying to get to this place of peace and purpose. Not everybody is gonna be an entrepreneur or make it to what we call the top. It's hard. It's a lot of work, not only in the physical but also in the spiritual. But what we all do have is purpose, and you, at some point, have to believe in yourself. Just imagine being the only one in your family to say, "I want to own my own business. I have no money, no resources on how, but I have a dream, and through hard work, discipline, sacrifice, pain, and tons of losses, my dreams came true."

I can honestly say, as I write this book, I'm so proud of myself for my strength, my tenacity, and my relationship with God. I've learned to include Him in everything. I can't do anything without him. When I look back over my 47 years of life, I've seen a lot and done a lot through the grace of God. I'm so truly grateful for His mercy. He kept me through my mess. Now, I'm enjoying the after-climb, no more pressure of proving or wanting anything but what God has for me. Simplicity is so peaceful. I get it. We have goals and aspirations. We really think it's about the climb, and it is, until you reach your top. And to be honest, there are not a lot of people you know already there, so now you have to go and meet new people because some of your old people don't know how to behave, so you end up leaving them behind. Then you realize it is the simple things of life. It really is the little things, and they are FREE and don't COST a thing.

You don't have to do anything but be open to new beginnings. Trust that God has a plan for your life. You are here for a purpose. We must seek that purpose, and when you do, you will see that getting out of alignment brings on so much pressure that we actually put on ourselves. Trust God. Trust yourself, and you will make it to a place called after the climb.

Good luck! Remember to slow down, smell some roses, pat yourself on the back, cheer yourself on, and even if you don't get what you want, give yourself some grace. You did a great JOB! You weathered many storms. You should be feeling very confident about everything that you experienced or are gonna experience. You should be able to explain why you think you had to go through it or why you are going through it. It takes some deep soul searching to get clarity. Most people think entrepreneurs don't get scared or feel insecure. We do. Actually, probably more than others. We already know people are gonna question our abilities. That's why it's so important that you let God do it. Let him fight your battles. We do things scared. We don't let fear stop us. We understand that you won't know until you try!

CHAPTER 7

WHO DO YOU THINK YOU ARE?

I'm free to be me, free of the pressures of success, free of proving my character. I have absolutely nothing else to prove that what is meant for me will not pass me by. I will no longer exhaust myself to have what we as the people call success. I have plenty of seeds in the ground. My job is to authentically be myself, and that should come pretty easily and effortlessly when it's real. You will and should feel a sense of freedom, peace, and, finally, alignment, some say in my lane. Before, we thought we had to make it happen, and it was all part of the plan. We had something to prove. We wanted the bag. As the younger generation says, we are chasing the bag. I can smile and encourage them to not overwork themselves, slow down and smell the roses, don't be in a rush, and take their time.

Everything has an appointed time. Sometimes, we can avoid some tough situations by listening and learning from those who have already done the hard part for us. You can learn from their mistakes. I remember my grandma used to tell me, "God already knows the plans He has for you." As a kid and even as an adult, you don't begin to understand until you have no one you can call on but GOD. There, in that place of brokenness, is where you develop a relationship where you learn to include Him in everything you are doing. Remember, He already knows you are trying to get to the place He has for you. Everybody's place will look different. The end results are the same, which is love, joy, peace, gratitude, and living life freely. There is no longer a bond of the pressures of reaching for the highest climb that you want to reach. God did it!

It reminds me of a diamond. A real diamond is formed deep within the earth under extreme pressure and temperature. You can also make diamonds. They are created in a controlled environment with added ingredients. Before I started including God, I was a lab diamond. I was adding all these ingredients I wanted for it to look like I wanted. When I was born, a diamond God had already equipped me with everything I needed. I had to learn to trust Him more than myself. Everything you need is already inside of you.

God, I thank You. He will keep you through all your self-inflicted wounds and all your insecurities. When I couldn't see my own worth, I was often reminded that God would pick me up and carry me the rest of the way. He did it for me. He will do it for you! We don't realize how God is keeping us from so much we can't see. I wanted that school so badly, but then over the years, every school that we had in my local area was closed due to some type of mismanagement of the financial aid. God did not want me to become the next. I could have easily become one. I showed you earlier that I wanted that money! So the next time God saved you from yourself, be humble and grateful and understand it could have been worse ... But God ... Trust His plans for you! I do!

AFTER THE CLIMB ... Who do you think you are?

Acknowledgments

I want to thank my mother, Diane Lyons, for her strength and her tough love, teaching me discipline. I've always admired her discipline skills, especially with money, that a lady can save a dollar. That's one skill I didn't get with the money. I wish. I also want to thank my stepfather, Carl Lyons. Carl came into our lives as a wonderful example of a father figure for both my daughter and me. She called him her grandpa. Thank you, Carl, for never complaining all the times I called you that I needed a ride from my girlfriend Cherry's house, and all the times you stood in the gap for my daughter when her dad or even I couldn't show up. You always did. I've always been truly grateful to have you to console me when I could not talk to my mother. You never took sides. I remember I surprised you one Father's Day with a Lexus 400. I used to listen to you talk about it, and I watched you admire that car. I was so excited to be able to surprise you with such a gift. You were so shocked. I had the man who sold it to me put a big red bow on it, too. God had blessed me to be able to be a blessing to you, and I was happy to oblige. You deserved it, paid in full! And y'all looked good in it. I love y'all!

I want to thank William Ward for allowing me to use his platform, which gave me an opportunity to become a salon owner. That opportunity changed my life, and it allowed me to give other people opportunities for their lives to change as well. Thank you!

I'm forever grateful.

I want to thank my best friend of 30-plus years, Cherriece. We call her Cherry. You and I are never apart. We met in high school. We are one. I have never met a woman like you. We were little girls when I first felt so connected to you. We know each other's thoughts when we look at the same picture. We know what we are thinking. We have our own language. We have our own look that nobody else knows about. We may burst out laughing and are the only two who know what we're laughing at.

Friendship is not about perfection. It's about forgiveness. It's about unconditional love. We went through some tough phases in our friendship. Cherry has always been my ride or die. I can trust her. I love her. We don't have any masks. We hold each other accountable.

We don't care if we get mad. We say what we are gonna say, and we know it's all done out of love. That's what has maintained our friendship for 30 years—unconditional love and forgiveness. We're not perfect. I'm not perfect. She's not perfect. The key is being able to discuss what we feel, not to point fingers or blame, but to come to a common ground that accommodates both perspectives so that we can move

ACKNOWLEDGMENTS

forward. That's how our friendship has survived 30-plus years. I don't agree with everything she does. She doesn't agree with everything I do, and we don't hide our feelings about how we feel. We are authentically connected through honesty and transparency. I love you, Bookie.

Read More!

Are you Ready To Climb.. Here's two of my Ebooks that you can instantly create income for your climb.

Click the pay links below.

Thank you for your support !

https://pay.beautyprofitcoaching.com/
d41b54f7-e26d-41dc-82cb-0eb

READ MORE!

KEISHA HUNTER
MINDSET & MONEY MAKE OVER

BUILDING YOUR WEALTH MINDSET

https://pay.beautyprofitcoaching.com/852cdd2c-6764-4f8e-95a1-028

About the Author

Keisha is a resilient entrepreneur whose journey began as a determined teen mom with big dreams. Balancing new motherhood with her pursuit of purpose, she transformed early challenges into fuel tor growth. Keisha built her first salon from the ground up , driven by desire to create generational change and inspire others facing similar obstacles. Today, she's a passionate mentor, speaker, and founder dedicated to empowering women to rewrite their stories. Keisha's work centers on confidence financial independence, and authentic leadership. Her voice reminds young mothers everywhere that how your start does not determine how far you can go.

URGENT PLEA!

Thank you for reading my book!
I really appreciate all of your feedback, and
I love hearing what you have to say.

I need your input to make the next version of this
book (and my future books) better.

Please take two minutes now to leave a helpful review on Amazon letting me know what you thought of the book.

Thanks so much!

-Keisha L. Hunter

selfpublishing.com

Selfpublishing.com helped me, and now I want them to help you with this **FREE book outline template!**

Even if you're busy, bad at writing, or
don't know where to start,
you CAN write a bestseller and build your best life.

With tools and experience across a
variety of niches and professions,
Selfpublishing.com is the only resource you need to take your book to the finish line!

DON'T WAIT.

Say "YES" to becoming a bestseller:
https://selfpublishing.com/friend/

www.ingramcontent.com/pod-product-compliance
Lightning Source LLC
Chambersburg PA
CBHW050517100526
44581CB00001B/2